AYDON CA

NORTHUMBERLA

D0231907

Henry Summerson

Aydon Castle is an outstanding example of a thirteenth-century English manor house. It was originally built in the 1290s as an undefended residence by Robert de Raymes, a wealthy Suffolk landowner who had moved to a then peaceful Northumberland. But no sooner had he arrived than war broke out in the borders, so that his new home, originally intended to proclaim his status among his neighbours, quickly had to be fortified for its owner's protection. Pillaged and burnt by the Scots in 1315, it was seized and robbed again by English rebels two years later. These misfortunes have left their mark on the house. The Raymes family went into decline from around 1400, and were bought out in 1541. Converted into a farmhouse in the seventeenth century, Aydon remained in occupation until 1966, but has survived little altered from its original state.

Main gate

❖ CONTENTS ❖

Aydon Castle, Corbridge, Northumberland, NE45 5PJ. Tel no: 01434 632450.

Visit our website at www.english-heritage.org.uk
Published by English Heritage,
1 Waterhouse Square, 138-142 Holborn, London EC1N 2ST
Copyright © English Heritage 2004

First published by English Heritage 2004, reprinted 2010, 2012, 2014
Edited by Patricia Briggs. Designed by Hoop Design. Picture research by Elaine Willis.
Photography by Keith Best and Jonathan Bailey. Plans and map by Richard Morris.
Printed by Graphius.

C20, 07/14, 04153, ISBN 978 1 85074 850 2
Photographs are copyright English Heritage unless otherwise stated.

TOUR OF THE CASTLE

INTRODUCTION

Aydon Castle is a wonderful survival from the middle ages. It is also a memorial to one of the most disastrous miscalculations in the history of English real estate. The name Aydon is both old and peaceful, combining two Old English words that probably mean 'hay pasture'. Aydon was acquired shortly after 1290 by a Suffolk landowner, Robert de Raymes, who had decided to move from the south to Northumberland. The site must have seemed a good one for a mansion, enjoying the natural defences created by the curve of the Ay Burn (as it was then known) immediately behind it, as well as easy access (the region's main east-west road is just three miles south at Corbridge, and the old road into Scotland, known as Dere Street, is just a few miles to the west). At the end of the thirteenth century, the county had been largely at peace for over seventy years, and Robert must have thought it was going to stay that way. But at the time he set about building his new residence at Aydon, centuries of intermittent Anglo-Scottish conflict

began. This explains certain ambiguities in the form that Aydon eventually took, and also its status: it is recorded more often as Aydon Hall than as Aydon Castle. Its position near the England–Scotland border meant that it had to have some of the attributes of a fortress, in the shape of walls and battlements, but it was actually planned as a manor house, with all the amenities of a gentleman's residence. It was the centre, too, of a farming estate, growing crops and pasturing livestock, and remained so, under changing ownership, from the late fourteenth century until 1966 – more often than not it was leased to a tenant farmer. In 1966, the castle was placed in the guardianship of the Ministry of Works, and since 1984 it has been in the care of English Heritage. As you go round, you will come across evidence for the castle's domestic and agricultural use, like glimpses of civilian clothes under a military uniform.

View of Aydon from the east, over fields whose produce would once have maintained the castle's occupants

❖ STAGES OF CONSTRUCTION ❖

Most of what you see at Aydon was built in about twenty years, between approximately 1295 and 1315. When Robert de Raymes arrived, he probably found nothing more elaborate than a wooden hall. His own building operations are likely to have begun with the solar block set across the east end of that hall. The garderobe block, which projects from the south-east corner of the solar, was also part of this first stage of his plan of works. This was followed by the present hall, which had a small kitchen at its west end. Quite possibly this (A) was all that Robert originally intended to build. But then, as the threat of war grew and, with it, the possibility that Aydon would need a garrison and defensible walls, a much larger kitchen, with plenty of ground-level storage space, replaced the first one. Projecting from the original kitchen's north wall, this second kitchen, with the addition of two short walls, created a battlemented courtyard in front of the entrance to the house (B). Finally, further lodgings were built off the old kitchen's west end, and the whole complex was surrounded by a curtain wall, so creating a large courtyard outside the inner one (C). All this was probably completed by 1315, when Robert de Raymes himself described Aydon as 'his dwelling…lately battlemented with a wall of stone and lime…'.

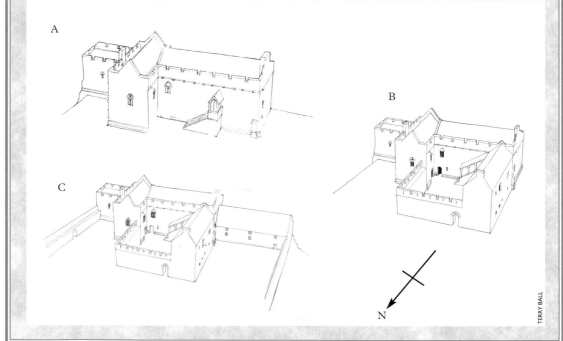

A

C

B

N

TERRY BALL

The tour begins ouside the main gate.

ENTRANCE

The lie of the land at Aydon means that you approach the castle as an attacker would have done, from the north. Before you enter at the main gate, pause to look round the corner to the right, where you will see a few machicolations (openings that would have allowed defence of the base of the wall; see p.23) – evidence that this was more than just an enclosing wall. Beneath is a blocked-up window and, next to it, a blocked-up postern (sub-sidiary doorway), which would have given access to the path up to the castle when the main gate was shut. The original wooden beams of the door are still clearly visible inside. To the left of the main gate you can see the outlet from a garderobe (latrine) in the wall. The gate itself could hardly be plainer; there was never a gatehouse, barbican, or any other form of defensive outworks essential to ward off determined besiegers.

The castle's outer gateway, looking through to the gateway to the inner courtyard

Archers could have shot down from the tower whose semicircular base you can see to the left, but neither that nor the ditch that once extended in front of the north wall could have kept attackers at bay for very long. So, even before you go inside, it is apparent that Aydon was a fortified manor house, not a fortress. But it was a manor house that could hold a lot of people.

Below: The outlet for a garderobe, with the remains of another visible behind it, which once served the lodgings on the other side of the wall

Below left: The blocked-up doorway and window in the outer wall, viewed from the outer courtyard

View across the outer courtyard to the remains of the mid-fourteenth-century tower

Enter the outer courtyard through the main gate.

OUTER COURTYARD

Once inside, you would originally have found the wall on either side of the

The nineteenth-century stables

entrance concealed by lodgings, which could have accommodated servants, or, in times of crisis, members of an enlarged garrison. Looking ahead, you can see another, smaller courtyard, also enclosed in a wall. Defensive in purpose, it was also intended to impress, in a manner characteristic of much medieval architecture, by creating a sequence of entrances.

To your right are nineteenth-century stables, perhaps replacing earlier ones. Horses were essential for transport, making a stable the medieval equivalent of a garage. It is thought that somewhere in this outer courtyard there was also once a well (the water

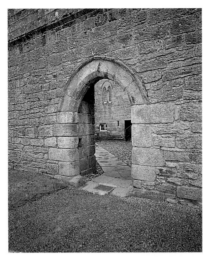

Far left: The entrance to the basement of the mid-fourteenth-century tower

Left: The elegant doorway into the inner courtyard

Below: The stairs up from the inner courtyard to the entrance to the hall. Note the rooflines cut into the wall above the stair

supply was recorded in this part of the castle in the nineteenth century), but its exact location is unknown. Across to your left, you can see the entrance to a chamber at the foot of the wall tower; it looks like a dungeon, but was probably built to hold stores. In the nineteenth century it housed a blacksmith's shop.

Go through the entrance to the inner courtyard.

INNER COURTYARD

Even now there is yet another stage to pass before you can enter the castle buildings, this time up a flight of stairs. The existing stairway dates from the sixteenth century, but it replaced an earlier one. Originally there was a porch at the top, where visitors could wait for admission (you can see the sharply pointed outline of its roof on the wall), but this was soon replaced by a lean-to that covered the whole length of the stair (the roof outline of this, too, is clearly visible).

BRITISH LIBRARY, MS EGERTON 3307, FOL. 72V

Above: A medieval party in progress, from a mid-fifteenth-century manuscript

Right: The hall seen from its west end, as it would have looked to a visitor entering from the screen

Below: The sixteenth-century stone screen at the west end of the hall

Go up the stairs and enter the screens area.

SCREEN

A screen – made of stone now, but originally wooden – separated the hall on the left, where meals were eaten, from the service rooms on the right, where they were prepared. In part, the division was dictated by convention, but the screen also prevented diners in the hall being disturbed by the movement of people and goods – at first, supplies for the kitchen probably came up the stairs, just as visitors did.

Turn left and enter the hall.

HALL

For outsiders, the hall was the social centre of the whole complex, where the lord appeared in public, particularly

when he entertained guests. He and his family would have sat at the far end, at a table extending across the hall, lit by the windows on either side, and facing the screen. Guests most likely sat at tables stretching down the hall from either end of the lord's table. There is no fireplace; warmth probably came from a fire in the centre of the room, either in a brazier or on a stone hearth. The open roof above is not original, but must have replaced one very like it, giving space for the smoke to rise and escape through a louvre at the top. A flat ceiling would have kept the smoke in and risked choking the diners. As it was, the walls, which would have been plastered and decorated either with paintings or hangings, must have been in constant need of cleaning because of the effects of smoke. Looking down the hall towards the screen, you can see

above it the fireplace of a room above. This was originally a gallery where musicians could play, and from which a steward or senior servant could observe the meal, keep an eye on the servants, and have food and drink taken in when necessary.

Return to the screen and go across into the original kitchen.

ORIGINAL KITCHEN

This was the first of three kitchens to be built at Aydon, and part of Robert de Raymes's first programme of works here. The fireplace stands where the oven once stood, with a cupboard cut into the wall immediately to its left, and a chute for getting rid of slops and rubbish next to the window. The window still holds its original iron grilles. In the small adjoining chamber on the left (perhaps a store) you can see the remains of the earlier wooden screen at floor level. It was probably the Carnabys – the castle's sixteenth-century owners – who put up the stone screen, just as they also inserted the fireplace, above which is carved their coat of arms.

SECOND KITCHEN

Return to the screens and turn left to enter the second kitchen.

The fourteenth-century fireplace in the first kitchen

Aydon's second kitchen was probably built soon after the first. Robert de Raymes was heavily involved in the fighting that broke out in the Borders after 1296, and needed more men, both to follow him to war and to defend his house. The original kitchen was too small to provide for them, so he built a new one, still with easy access to the hall. It was divided into two rooms, indicated by the change in floor level. The first was where food was prepared, both for cooking and serving, and where dishes were washed up afterwards – the water was disposed of in the sink in the left-hand corner.

The cooking took place in the second room, using seasonings stored in the cupboards cut into the walls. On the left, in the west wall, is another chute for waste – this time at floor level – to

The coat of arms of the Carnaby family over the fireplace

❖ MEDIEVAL KITCHENS AND COOKERY ❖

Medieval kitchen fireplaces were often very wide, because they had to be able to cook several things at once. Cooks used the cauldron more than the spit, and prepared soups and stews more often than whole roasted oxen or barons of beef. Bread was the basis of everyone's diet, rich and poor alike, but the rich were far more likely to eat meat as well, served on slabs of bread, or 'trenchers', which soaked up the gravy. Vegetables were more often eaten in pottages than by themselves. A principal reason for eating so much stewed food was that, in the absence of refrigeration, meat and fish were commonly preserved by smoking, salting or soaking in brine. Slow cooking in water softened the food,

while the addition of herbs and spices improved its flavour. Ale, home-brewed from oats or barley, was the commonest drink for everyone.

Cooking in a medieval kitchen, from a mid-fourteenth-century manu-script. A cauldron and turnspit are being used, along with a very long-handled spoon, to baste the meat

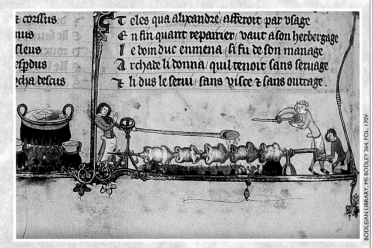

BODLEIAN LIBRARY, MS BODLEY 264, FOL. 170V

keep the kitchen clean of scraps. Next to this is a locked wooden door. When this kitchen was in use, food no longer came in through the inner courtyard but was brought directly into the kitchen through this door, perhaps hauled up on a rope or, more likely, carried up an outside staircase of wood, long vanished. The stonework to the right of the door shows that a large window was originally set here, like the one opposite, but was later replaced by the small window you see today, probably for greater security.

At the far end is the large fireplace where the cooking was done (it may have been moved here from the first kitchen). Its chimney has long vanished, as has the hood that once covered it, although its base is still visible and you can also see some of the hood stones above. Note the low stone benches on either side of the hearth; these may have been used to keep food and dishes warm, but could also have acted as seats for watchmen coming cold off duty, or for cooks keeping an eye on a meal's progress.

This kitchen went out of use in the sixteenth century, when another one was designed on the far side of the castle. The floors became unsafe and the room was deserted, except by pigeons. The series of holes cut into the stones around the top of this room was added in the nineteenth century to pro-vide nesting boxes for the pigeons, which got in through holes in the inner-courtyard wall. (The pigeons were valued for their meat, not as racers.)

Go through the doorway in the corner and out onto the wall-walk.

WALL-WALK AND BATTLEMENTS

In the middle ages, the kitchen was also the point of access to the defences of the inner courtyard. From the wall-walk, you can see how the finely made battlements alternate with arrow-slits, but, to anyone attacking, the top of the wall would have looked very different, because gaps between battlements were covered with wooden hoardings (the model in the ground-floor rooms under the hall shows how they would have looked). From the wall-walk there are fine views north towards Halton.

Looking back at the house, you can see the guttering and spouts that carried off rainwater, and, above them, more battlements. (The latter, however, must have been essentially ornamental, as there is no stair up to them, there is hardly space for a man to stand behind them, and they continue round on the south side, which overlooks the river valley and

The west wall of the second kitchen, showing storage cupboard, waste chute in the floor, and the outline of the blocked window beyond the doorway

The fireplace at the north end of the second kitchen, with the doorway to the wall-walk next to it

Doublet-lancet window with the head of God the father over the lights; this may have been carved for a chapel that was never built

so was safe from attack.) As you go along the wall-walk to the end, notice in the north-facing wall the twin-light window, with its elegant pointed arches and the carved head above them. This is possibly God the father, as carved for a chapel that was never built. Around the window can be seen the little holes that once held iron grilles (like those still present in the first kitchen); these were an elementary safety device that would hardly have deterred the Scots, but might have kept out local thieves. The same holes can be seen on several other windows, some of which also had internal shutters.

As you go back through the kitchen, look up above the door connecting it to its predecessor. You can see a door, reached by a now-lost wooden stair, that gave access to the gallery overlooking the hall and, later, to the room that succeeded it.

Return to the hall, and go through the arch in the far right-hand corner.

As you go through into the upstairs solar, notice how badly the walls of the hall and the solar fit together to the right of the archway. The solar was probably built to join an earlier hall, which may have been made of wood. The hall was then replaced by the existing structure and either the work was done hastily, or the builders lacked skill and left signs of their incompetence.

View over the inner courtyard from the wall-walk, showing the decorative battlements above the hall

Originally, however, the clumsy join would have been hidden by wall plaster.

UPSTAIRS SOLAR

Used as the lord's private apartments, the upstairs solar (a word apparently derived from the Latin word *solus*, meaning alone or unaccompanied) is laid out as a single large room, but probably was formerly divided in two. To your left, in the north wall, you can see a blocked-up doorway next to the two-light window you saw from the wall-walk. Originally, this was the private entrance for the lord and his family, reached from outside by a wooden staircase near where the courtyard wall now stands. This staircase was most likely abandoned, and the door blocked, as a security measure. Thereafter, the solar was reached either through the hall or by

stairs from the room below.

To give privacy, the room was divided by a partition, seemingly where the head of the present staircase stands. The smaller, southern part of the solar might then have served as a lobby or waiting room for visitors, although it is easy to imagine that members of the family also enjoyed its window seat and its view over the ravine, especially in summer. The main room was the northern one, with its fireplace and its three windows, also with seats. The fireplace was originally set in the opposite wall (you can see the marks it left on the stonework) but was moved across the room by the Carnabys, perhaps in the hope that it would also warm the hall on the other side of the wall. It is also possible that since its previous position was immediately above the fireplace downstairs, smoke

Above left: The doorway from the hall into the solar block

Above: The fireplace in the solar, awkwardly set into the wall opposite the one against which it originally stood

in the latter's chimney-flue leaked from it into the solar's fireplace. In any case the move was rather clumsily done, and the fireplace now stands lower than it should, looking decidedly top-heavy.

Cross the solar and turn left through a doorway into the garderobe.

Upstairs garderobe

The position and amenities of this chamber suggest that this was the lord's bedchamber. Lit by windows on three sides (the one in the south wall, on your right, is a later replacement), it was, in effect, a medieval en suite. Notice the small cupboard cut into the wall at the far end, and the chute next to it, for washing water. The latrine itself is a double-decker, for there is a similar arrangement below; this upper one is set further back to prevent accidents. In the 1920s this chamber became a bathroom (you can still see the lead piping), but by then the medieval latrine had been superseded by an earth closet in the kitchen garden.

Return to the solar and go down the stairs.

The staircase is almost all that is left of the fittings that were in use up to 1966. It is probably nineteenth-century, although it seems likely that there was always a staircase hereabouts.

Turn left and left again at the bottom of the stairs.

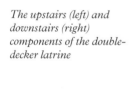

The upstairs (left) and downstairs (right) components of the double-decker latrine

The downstairs solar, looking toward its sixteenth-century fireplace

DOWNSTAIRS GARDEROBE

In the nineteenth century this was used as a dairy, with a store for barrels of beer against its back wall – on the floor you can still see the blocks used to hold them in place.

Return to the downstairs solar.

DOWNSTAIRS SOLAR

There are three doorways in the west wall of this room. You can see that the door on the far right opens onto the inner courtyard; this may have been added when the outside stair up to the solar on the floor above was removed. Before then the chamber was only accessible from above, suggesting that it was a retreat for the lord's family, perhaps in winter. The windows were smaller – the two that have survived from the years around 1300 are little more than lancets – and the room was warmed by the handsome fireplace in the centre of the east wall, decorated with a row of carved bosses.

In the sixteenth century this room was converted into yet another kitchen, as the Carnabys abandoned the original kitchen in the west wing. For cooking they installed the fire - place in the corner, with a recess for baking bread at its left end. In the nineteenth century, after the castle had become a farmhouse, the main fireplace was adapted for cooking; it held an iron stove, later replaced by an Aga oven. The south end of the chamber was then used as the family dining room.

The downstairs solar's handsome original fireplace, of around 1300

The lintel of the doorway into the downstairs solar from the inner courtyard, carved with the initials of William and Henry Collinson and the year 1653

The fine stone vault of the stores under Robert de Raymes's second kitchen. Notice the 'shouldered' arch, characteristic of the early fourteenth century, at the far end

ROOMS UNDER THE HALL

The other two doors in the west wall of the downstairs solar give access to what was originally another single open-spaced chamber, with the same outline as the hall above. In the sixteenth century or later, however, it was divided into the series of rooms you see today.

The right-hand doorway leads into a small room that may have originated as a porter's lodge; in the nineteenth century it served as a pantry. The left-hand doorway leads into what became the drawing room. The pair of nineteenth-century French windows gave access to a south-facing veranda. The medieval fireplace (now with much later fittings) situated in the next room indicates that this must have been intended to provide accommodation when necessary – when the garrison was built up, or when Aydon received visitors. From here there is a doorway through to a passageway, which was used to store coals in the nineteenth century. Another doorway immediately opposite (now blocked-up) led through to a room which was, successively, part of the stabling and then a wash-house.

Retrace your steps to the downstairs solar, go out into the inner courtyard and cross the courtyard to enter the block of stores under the second kitchen.

As you leave the downstairs solar, look back at the lintel above the doorway, where you can see the initials of William Collinson – who bought Aydon in the mid-seventeenth century – together with the date, and the initials of his son Henry.

STORES AND STABLES

The doorway here has a 'shouldered' arch, which was the characteristic shape for doorways built around 1300. There are examples of it all over the castle; as you step inside you will see two more examples to left and right.

These three interconnected rooms were built to hold stores for the kitchens immediately above, but were later converted into stables and cowsheds, with feeding troughs for the animals and drains to carry the muck away. As you enter the middle store, notice the garderobe in the wall opposite. This complex particularly impressed eighteenth-century visitors, who noted that no timber had been used in their construction and admired the fine vault in the chamber at the south end. The chamber at the north end is also vaulted. The conversion of this block was the work of William Collinson, whose initials are again carved outside on the lintel above the doorway at the north end, with the date 1657. It may have been when this door was opened up that the chimney stack for the kitchen fireplace on the floor above was demolished.

Leave the stable block through the doorway at the north end to emerge into the outer courtyard.

The west walls of the second kitchen and the hall; the outline of the gable of Robert de Raymes's lodgings block is clearly visible on the latter

The 'tusking stones' on the east wall of the solar block, where further building was planned but never started

View of the castle across the orchard, showing the solar block's two chimneys and the projecting garderobe block

EXTERNAL FEATURES

Turn left into the middle courtyard on the other side of the block you have just gone through.

At the far end are the remains of more lodgings built by Robert de Raymes – you can see the outline of their pointed roof on the west wall of the hall block. A two-storey building on the side of the castle safest from attack, its windows had double lights, even at ground level.

Return to the inner courtyard and go through the doorway leading to the orchard.

ORCHARD

This used to be the kitchen garden; it was converted to growing fruit only in 1941. You get a good view here of the east wall of the solar block, with its two sturdy chimneys. The one to the left, faced with cut stone, formed part of Robert de Raymes's original structure. Its workmanship is clearly superior to that of the smaller chimney to the right, built by the Carnabys for their new kitchen. Notice too the exterior of the added bread oven on the corner.

   On the north-east corner of the solar block you can see a number of projecting stones, known as 'tusking stones', indicating that Robert de Raymes at one time planned a building here. It is possible, although there is no firm evidence for this, that he wanted to have his own chapel here, as he had done in his manor house in Suffolk (the nearest parish church otherwise is in Corbridge), and that this was the site he chose for it. The carved head in the solar window just round the corner could originally have been made to decorate it. The addition was never built, however – perhaps the money ran out, or perhaps Scottish attacks created other priorities.

Go through the door in the outer wall.

OUTSIDE THE CURTAIN WALL

You can walk around the south side of the castle. Notice the two heavy buttresses supporting the east wall of the latrine block, which might otherwise be dangerously close to the edge of the valley. Looking up at this wall, you can see two chutes at the top for rainwater from the roof, and two further chutes for waste water from inside each of the chambers on the two floors below. And if you look at the larger of the buttresses, you can see the outlet from the latrines, skilfully placed to deposit waste in the ravine below.

Continuing along the path will bring you to the south end of the solar block – also buttressed to help it stay in place – and then to the outer wall of the hall block. In the nineteenth century and later there were gardens here, and early photographs show members of the Rowell family sitting outside the French windows, no doubt enjoying the view over the spectacular drop into the valley below, long known as 'Jack's (or Jock's) Leap'. In the eighteenth century, Jack was thought to have been an unhappy lover, who threw himself over the edge when spurned by his lady-love. But for later generations this was too tame an explanation, and tales were told of a border reiver, or civil war soldier, who with a single heroic bound jumped to freedom in the dell below. There is no reason to believe that either of these stories is true, but fortunately Aydon hardly needs such romantic embellishments.

A few more steps will bring you to one of the castle's most noteworthy features: the graceful chimney built around 1300 for the fireplace under the hall. A simple circular shaft, with outlets for smoke at the top, it illustrates perfectly the high quality of the fittings provided for the original manor house.

Continue round to a doorway leading back into the middle courtyard.

The superb chimney for the fireplace to the lower hall, on the castle's south side

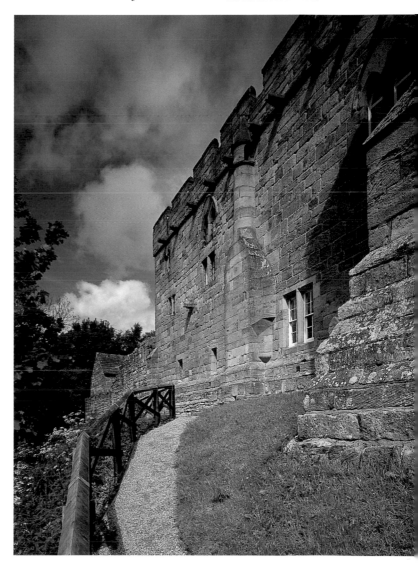

HISTORY OF THE CASTLE

THE EARLY HISTORY OF AYDON

An illuminated page from Alice de Raymes's early-fourteenth-century book of hours

CAMBRIDGE UNIVERSITY LIBRARY, MS D.4.17

Although prehistoric and Roman remains have been found near Aydon, there is no certain evidence that the site of the castle was occupied before the thirteenth century. The name is first recorded in 1225, by which time the village had long formed part of the barony of Bolam. The barony comprised a compact lordship, stretching south-west from Bolam itself and nearby Belsay to Aydon and Little Whittington, just outside Corbridge. In 1207, Walter de Burun died without a male heir, and his barony was divided between his two daughters and their husbands. Both inherited lands at Aydon and, as a result, the village had two landlords throughout the middle ages; the site of the castle passed first to Alina de Cauz, and then to Alina's daughter Margaret. In 1246, Margaret married Richard de Gosebek, who took his name from Gosbeck in Suffolk. It was probably he who built whatever house preceded the later castle. But Hugh, the son of Richard and Margaret, clearly preferred to remain in Suffolk, for, sometime between 1284 (when his mother died) and 1296, he sold his share of the barony of Bolam to another Suffolk landowner, Hugh de Raymes, and Hugh's son Robert.

The Raymes family (the name, which until the mid-fourteenth century was usually spelt Reymes, probably derives from Rames near Lillebonne in Normandy) was long-established in Suffolk, and had accumulated a considerable estate in and around Ipswich, centred upon Wherstead, just south of that town. It is not known what Hugh paid for his Northumbrian half-barony, but it is recorded that his son

❖ ROBERT DE RAYMES ❖

Robert de Raymes's move to Northumberland was probably a result of both a taste for adventure and social ambition. His possession of Aydon made him technically a baron, while the outbreak of war with Scotland gave him the chance to make a reputation as a soldier, at a time when secular society placed military values above all others. He fought in Scotland in 1297 and 1298, and went there again in 1309 as an ambassador. He was probably captured in the great Scottish victory at Bannockburn on 24 June 1314; his ransom of 500 marks (£333.33), along with his alleged losses in Scottish raids, provides striking testimony to his wealth. Royal grants, including a yearly pension of £10 from the Newcastle customs, helped him to keep going afterwards. He served again in armies on the Borders, and he was one of the two knights of the shire who represented Northumberland in parliament in 1322. When he died, probably on 2 February 1324, he was still an important man in his adopted county; his tomb-effigy in Bolam church represents him as a knight in full armour.

The effigy of Robert de Raymes in Bolam church

had to pay a fine of £60 when it was discovered that the transaction had been completed without the king's consent (as the law required). This suggests that it was seen as a valuable property. Indeed, there is every reason why it should have been, in a part of England once regarded as remote and backward, but by the 1290s catching up fast with the rest of the country. When Hugh died in 1295 his Suffolk property passed to his niece Alice and her husband Robert of Reydon. Alice's book of hours survives (in Cambridge University Library), complete with some beautiful illuminations, one of which shows her kneeling before a bishop. Perhaps aesthetic tastes ran in the family, which could explain her cousin Robert's choice of Aydon, with its superb position, for his new home, and the fine detailing of the work he financed.

After showing solidarity with the barons and knights he had come to live among by fighting alongside them in the late 1290s, Robert de Raymes may have devoted his energies to his estates for a while. He sent substitutes for the Scottish campaign of 1300 rather than serving himself, perhaps so that he could supervise the building work at Aydon. By 1301 Robert was beginning to win a place for himself among the Northumbrian gentry. In that year he bought land – at both Aydon and

Dilston – and in 1304 he made provision for the descent of his properties, as was proper for a now-married man. His wife was Maud Wortley, whose mother was a member of the important Northumbrian family of Heron of Ford.

In 1305, Robert obtained a royal licence to crenellate, both at his other manor of Shortflatt, just south of Bolam, and at Aydon itself. (To crenellate a building was to add battlements and other marks of fortification.) This needed royal consent, in theory so that the king could control the spread of castles within his realm, but in practice so that he could take a fee from those who wanted the status of a castellated house. A licence to crenellate was more often granted when building works were finished, than before they were begun, and was very rarely refused. It is unlikely that Robert de Raymes suddenly decided in 1305 that Aydon had to be strengthened, for in the previous year Scottish resistance had effectively collapsed, to all outward appearances ending the war in the north. Perhaps he wanted a further chance to demonstrate his own wealth and importance.

AYDON UNDER ATTACK

The fortification of Aydon soon acquired a greater significance than Robert de Raymes intended. On 25 March 1306, Robert Bruce seized the

Building in progress, as represented in an early-fifteenth-century illuminated manuscript

BRITISH LIBRARY, MS ROY. 15. D.III, FOL. 15V

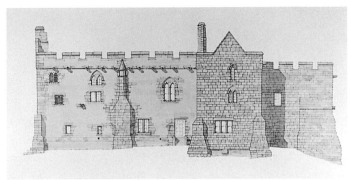

weapons (notably crossbows) and provisions worth £300. But he tamely came to terms with the Scots and surrendered, with the result that the castle was pillaged and burnt. In military terms, however, Hugh's judgement was probably sound; Aydon was simply not strong enough to resist an invading army, and his action constituted a revealing comment on its military significance. Two years later, Aydon suffered again, this time at English hands – indeed those of the same Hugh de Gales who had surrendered in 1315. As the Scots spread havoc in all directions the government of Northumberland effectively collapsed. In the resulting anarchy, Hugh and his followers seized Aydon on 5 December 1317, and during the following month, according to Robert de Raymes, they 'burnt, took and carried off the timber

Scottish throne. Then, on 7 July 1307, Edward I of England died. These events led directly to years of misery for the northern counties of England, as the Scots first drove the English out, and then conducted raid after raid over the border, looting and burning. Aydon was not spared. In 1311, and again in 1312, Corbridge and the surrounding area were laid waste by forces led by Bruce in person. Aydon's walls may have kept the enemy away on these occasions, but in 1315 there was no escape. In Robert de Raymes's absence, the defences were commanded by one Hugh de Gales. He had been entrusted, as Robert later complained bitterly, with a fortress fully equipped for defence and stocked with

Above: William Twopenny's mid-nineteenth-century drawing of the castle's south face, as it would have looked without shrubs and flowerbeds

Above left: The outer west wall of Aydon Castle, with machicolations above and a postern below, now blocked up

BRITISH LIBRARY, CO'T. CH. XIX. 4

The seal of Robert Bruce as king of Scots

Soldiers looting a house, as represented in a late-fourteenth-century manuscript

BRITISH LIBRARY

Aerial view of Aydon, showing how the castle is protected on three sides by the Ay (now Cor) Burn

and other goods and chattels, namely linen and woollen cloths, gold, silver, hangings, gold brooches and household utensils to the value of £200…'.

An inquest held after Robert's death records the ruin of his manors of Bolam, Shortflatt and Aydon itself. All were now worthless, for lack of livestock and tenants, thanks to destruction by the Scots. Northumberland continued to suffer from endemic disorder for the rest of the Middle Ages, periodically worsened by Scottish raids and even full-scale invasions. One such invasion took place in 1346. As an army led by King David II crossed the Pennines and headed for Corbridge, Aydon's position on Dere Street again placed it in the line of attack. And, although its defences had probably been strengthened since 1315 by the addition of the semi-circular tower to the north-facing curtain wall, the occupants nevertheless prudently took the line of least resistance and surrendered in return for their lives. (Significantly, the only contemporary report of this incident describes the little fortress as Aydon Hall, not Castle.) But, despite such hazards, Northumbrian society never broke down again as it had done in Edward II's reign (1307–27). Commerce and government resumed, and Robert de Raymes's son and heir – another Robert – took part in both. In 1347 he became sheriff of the county, and in 1348 he represented it in parliament, and is recorded as dealing in wool at Newcastle in the same year. Very little is known about the Raymes family finances, but this episode suggests that they did not regard trade as being beneath their dignity. It was by such means that Robert II maintained the position of his family as his father had established it.

THE ADVENTUROUS LIFE OF NICHOLAS DE RAYMES

Robert de Raymes II died of the Black Death in 1349, and was succeeded by his three sons in turn. Nicholas, the youngest of these, enjoyed probably a more successful career than any other member of the Raymes family, even though he was also decidedly prone to disorder and debt. Having gone on campaigns in France in 1355 and 1359, he got into trouble with the law at home in 1363, as an accessory to the murder of John Coupland – an important, though highly unpopular, royal official. As a consequence he spent some years in prison, and he succeeded to Aydon only in 1376, even though his elder brother Hugh had died about twelve years earlier. He was several times prosecuted for debt. Employed by Sir Henry Delaval as his receiver at Seaton Delaval, he failed to account for the money he had received, while the prior of Carlisle (who was rector of Corbridge, the parish in which Aydon stood) sued him for £50, suggesting that Nicholas had been refusing to pay tithes. In 1380, Nicholas became the king's escheator, an important financial official, for the northern counties, and again he failed to account for what he had collected.

Nicholas de Raymes had powerful friends, however – chief among whom was the greatest man in the county, Henry Percy, first Earl of Northumberland. Some time in the 1370s or 1380s, Nicholas followed the earl to war in Scotland with a force of thirty men.

A reconstruction drawing by Terry Ball of the lodgings in the middle courtyard.

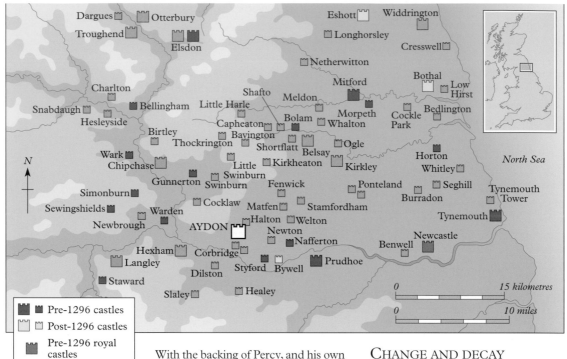

Map of the castles and towers of Tyndale and southern Northumberland, before and after the outbreak of the Anglo-Scottish wars in 1296

With the backing of Percy, and his own talents, he was able to get out of scrapes and even to obtain further employment in government. In 1378 and 1385 he represented Northumberland in parlia-ment, and he also became a Justice of the Peace, served as chamberlain of Berwick and keeper of Roxburgh Castle, and went on embassy to Scotland in 1390. The fact that Nicholas was able to arrange an excellent marriage for his son Robert – to a daughter of the highly influential Sir Robert Ogle – suggests that his wild ways were not held against him in the county, and when he died, in 1394, his family must have seemed set for still better things.

CHANGE AND DECAY

The fifteenth century proved a sad anticlimax, both for Aydon and its owners. Already in the late fourteenth century Nicholas de Raymes had been increasingly resident at Shortflatt, a move perhaps dictated by considerations of security. Aydon was too far south to be seriously affected by the activities of border reivers, but there was always the danger of a long-distance raid. In March 1386, English and Scottish bandits were alleged to have cooperated in seizing an Aydon man and taking him back to the border, where he was held to ransom. Now leased to tenants, in around 1415

Aydon was listed among the other Northumbrian fortresses that had proliferated since the beginning of the fourteenth century. Presumably it was then in working order, but in 1450 it was described as 'a ruinous castle', perhaps having been attacked during the short but fierce Anglo-Scottish war of 1448–9. The fortunes of the Raymes family were now equally ramshackle. They ceased to hold local offices, and they largely failed to make good marriages. They may have allied themselves with the Nevilles, who became lords of nearby Bywell in 1397, and so earned the hostility of the Percys, but it is equally likely that they simply lacked talent. Aydon seems to have continued to be occupied, but by tenants. In the early sixteenth century these were members of the Shafto family from Bavington (a few miles north-east of Hexham). Eventually, the eighth Robert de Raymes (Nicholas's great-great-grandson) decided to consolidate his estates, and made Aydon over to Sir Reynold Carnaby in exchange for lands at Hawkwell, much closer to Shortflatt. Sir Reynold, who was in the process of building up a substantial estate based on Hexham, then placed Aydon (described as a castle in the documents) in the hands of his brother Cuthbert.

The Carnabys made substantial internal changes at Aydon, especially to the kitchen and to the roofs – tree-ring tests have dated the timber in the roofs of the latrine block and the west-wing kitchen to the early 1540s. Cuthbert's sons bore the Arthurian names Lionel and Lancelot, and perhaps liked the idea of living in a castle, which is how Aydon appears on John Speed's map of Northumberland, published in 1612. But by now it was again in the hands of tenants – this time one Lionel Winshoppe, who was subsequently sued by Lancelot Carnaby for arrears of rent. But it was not difficulties with tenants that caused Aydon to change hands again. After the civil wars of the 1640s Ralph Carnaby was heavily penalised by parliament for supporting

A castle under siege, from a late-fourteenth-century manuscript

The roof of the west-wing kitchen, with timbers inserted by the Carnabys in the early 1540s

❖ THE DISCOVERY OF AYDON ❖

Accounts of Aydon begin in the late eighteenth century with John Wallis and William Hutchinson, who published accounts of Northumberland in 1769 and 1778 respectively. They regretted the ruin into which the castle had fallen, but admired its situation and also the stables in the west wing, perhaps the only structure then in use. But true appreciation of the castle's architectural importance began in 1851, when T H Turner published a brief account and a plan, accompanied by drawings by William Twopenny showing the chimney and various doors, windows and chimneys. The beauty of the castle's site also attracted attention, and in 1879 it was said to be 'much frequented by holiday visitors'. In the twentieth century, Aydon became increasingly well known, and was studied as a remarkable example of a late thirteenth-century gentleman's residence. Margaret Wood, writing in 1950, remarked that 'the building is important for its well-preserved, windows, chimney and fireplaces'; the dryness of her phrasing cannot conceal her fascinated absorption in what she found there.

Two views of Aydon from the south by William Twopenny, showing the whole castle (left), and the outside chimney (right)

BRITISH MUSEUM

BRITISH MUSEUM

Charles I. In 1654, he and his son (also Ralph) sold Aydon Castle – with an estate made up of 300 acres of arable land, 200 of meadow, 200 of pasture and 50 of wood – to William Collinson of Tynemouth, for £653. Collinson and his son Henry farmed their Aydon estate, but did not last long there, for in 1702 Henry Collinson sold up for £2350 to John Douglas, a man of humble origins who had prospered both as a lawyer and through his connections to the coal industry, and who was engaged in building up a large estate in Northumberland. In 1751 his granddaughter Anne married Sir Edward Blackett, and their descendants, living at Matfen, have owned Aydon ever since.

AYDON IN RECENT TIMES

Like so many previous owners, the Blacketts leased Aydon to tenants, but these do not always seem to have lived in the castle, which deteriorated badly. However, in the nineteenth century, things improved. There was a growing interest in, and appreciation of, things medieval, and perhaps it was this that led Sir Edward Blackett, the sixth baronet, to put the castle 'into a complete state of repair' after it had long been 'neglected and ruinous'. Probably this was around 1830. The castle was also once more used as a working farm, and the interior was reshaped to provide the necessary accommodation. Around the same

Early twentieth-century photograph of members of the Rowell family sitting on the verandah outside the French windows at the south end of the drawing room

*The kitchen garden on the
north side of the castle
around 1920, where the
orchard is now*

COUNTRY LIFE PICTURE LIBRARY

time, members of the local Rowell family came into occupation, and they stayed at Aydon for just over a century. Their children were both born and educated there; a schoolroom was installed on the first floor of the old latrine block, presided over by a governess. Water was pumped up from an underground spring and heated on the kitchen range; a maid carried it to the bedrooms in cans every morning. There was no bathroom or toilet before the 1920s, and no electricity until 1950, so oil lamps (later paraffin ones) and candles provided lighting. The farm reared cattle, sheep and pigs, and grew a variety of crops. In the nineteenth century, Irish labourers were hired to hoe turnips in the early summer, while during the Second World War, prisoners-of-war – both German and Italian – would come to pick potatoes under armed guard. As far as possible the farm was self-supporting – butter was made on the premises, for instance – but the Rowells seem to have lived well. They had books and pictures, and an Erard piano in the drawing room. Early photographs record a hard tennis court in the outer courtyard. The writer William Tomlinson, in a county guide published in 1889, described Aydon as 'a better-class farm-house, though still retaining many of its ancient features…'.

The Rowells probably lived beyond their means, and in any case farming became steadily less profitable throughout England in the early twentieth century. Robert Rowell – who had been born in the castle in 1853 – died in 1932, aged nearly 90. His eldest son, whom he expected to succeed to the tenancy, was killed shortly afterwards in a motorcycle accident, and the rest of the family left. Shortly after a new tenant had taken up residence, tragedy struck again, when two little children were suffocated by the smoke from a fire that broke out in one of the bedrooms fitted into the medieval hall. Aydon acquired the reputation of an unlucky farm, and it became difficult to find tenants. It made little money, and the roofs needed constant attention. Finally, in 1966, Sir Charles Blackett, the ninth baronet, placed the castle in the guardianship of the Ministry of Works, which proceeded to conduct a thorough restoration, albeit one that involved removing practically all the nineteenth-century fittings. Consequently, it is chiefly as a remarkable survival from the years around 1300 that Aydon is still valued today.

FURTHER READING

Dixon, P (1988) *Aydon Castle*.

Dixon, P (1992) 'From hall to tower', *in* Coss, P R and Lloyd, S D (eds) *Thirteenth Century England* IV, 85–107

Craster, H H E (ed) (1914) *A history of Northumberland* 10, Newcastle upon Tyne, 333–66

Knowles, W H (1899) 'Aydon Castle, Northumberland'. *Archaeologia* 56, 71–88

Oliver, H (1996) *Aydon castle in the 1920s*, Hexham Local History Society

Parker, J H and Turner, T H (1851) *Domestic architecture of the middle ages 1*, 148–9

Pevsner, N and others (2002) *The Buildings of England: Northumberland*, 3rd edn

Raimes, A L (1954) 'Shortflatt Tower and its owners'. *Archaeologia Aeliana* 4.32, 126–59

Raimes, F (1908) 'Robert de Reymes of Bolam, Shortflatt and Aydon Castle, and his connexion with Suffolk'. *Archaeologia Aeliana*, 3.4, 313–18

Wood, M E (1950) 'Thirteenth-century domestic architecture'. *Archaeological Journal* 105, supplement

The author also benefited greatly from the recorded reminiscences of the late Mr Herbie Snelgar, the last occupant of Aydon Castle when it was a working farm.

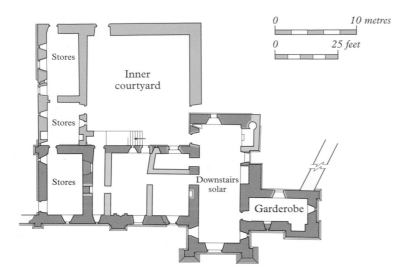

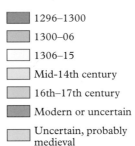

Main buildings: ground floor

	1296–1300
	1300–06
	1306–15
	Mid-14th century
	16th–17th century
	Modern or uncertain
	Uncertain, probably medieval

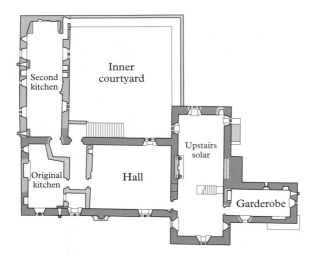

Main buildings: first floor